Feed My Sheep

Teachings for Pastors

ISBN-13: 978-1-938520-11-2

Feed My Sheep / Pastor Star R. Scott—1st ed.

Feed My Sheep

Teachings for Pastors

by Pastor Star R. Scott

Table of Contents

.

Publisher's Note

The work you hold in your hands is a compilation of sermon transcripts that Pastor Star R. Scott has delivered to his Sterling, Virginia congregation during forty years of ministry there. While using segments of transcriptions is certainly not the most commonformat for a published work, the possibility of doing so was approached with care and deliberation.

In recent years, with the republication of older Christian literature, some publishers have taken considerable license in editing the writing of great authors who have since gone home to be with the Lord. This seems to have been done in the interest of making the writings more palatable for today's Christian reader. Because of our interest in maintaining the integrity of the doctrine and even retaining the anointing that was on these messages as they were originally delivered, we have decided to present them here in transcribed form.

Perhaps the most direct admonition to take this approach came from one of the great pioneers of the Pentecostal movement in the twentieth century, Willard Cantelon. Cantelon, who was truly an eloquent man, and mighty in the scriptures, considered Pastor Scott to be his spiritual pastor and dear friend. In a personal letter to Scott, Cantelon encouraged him: "I am sure that recording your sermons on tape is one of the 'wisest' things you do. And knowing that these messages can be transcribed in writing and find their way to the different 'levels' of readers in the days ahead is a long-range vision that is most real." In another letter, Cantelon continued by saying, "There is something special about what is delivered 'live' and printed the way it is given." We certainly agree with Brother Cantelon's perspective on these matters and therefore present these timely yet timeless teachings in such a format.

As you prepare for the soon return of our Lord and seek to strengthen your relationship with Father, we pray that you will be helped, challenged, and enriched by these teachings.

Principles for
Godly Leadership

Chapter 1

Return to the Old Paths

"Thus saith the Lord, Stand ye in the ways, and see,
and ask for the old paths, where is the good way, and
walk therein, and ye shall find rest for your souls"
(*King James Version,* Jeremiah 6:16).

Would you like to pastor a million people? You can have it!
That's too big a headache for me! One thing you'll notice
is different about our ministry is that we don't talk about how big a
church is but about how pure it is. I have found that "large" and "pure"
don't always go together. The straight and narrow path is one few find.
Now, "few" is a relative term, and God does add to the church as He
sees fit. It's not how many you have; it's how many the Lord added.

Maybe you don't need to add more people; many of you need to subtract.
Have you ever heard of a church subtraction conference? Church growth
conferences typically emphasize "bigger is better." I want to tell you
something: better is better. As Americans, we think big has to be better.
It must be fancy, expensive—have to wear my $1,500 suit, my big gold
watch, drive my Mercedes. I could jump, sweat, yell, and raise money by the
boatload, but is that what the ministry is all about? I'm sick of it! It's not a
gospel the apostle Paul would recognize. It's time to return to the old paths.

A number of years ago, our ministry was the hottest thing in
Washington, D.C. We witnessed the dead being raised, blind eyes
being opened, and the lame walk as a result of God moving in our
meetings. People were coming from around the world to our meetings
for us to lay hands on them. Known as a man of faith, I was asked

at that time to address thousands of pastors at a church growth conference. The leader of the conference asked me to teach on the subject of faith for church growth. Seated beside me on the platform were the premiere evangelical ministers of the day. As I looked around at all these pastors, something went off in my spirit. It was as though I could see into the hearts of these men, and I heard these words in my spirit: "Tell me how to be a success. These other men seem to be successes. How can I be a success?"

I stood before those men and heard the words come out of my mouth. They didn't start in my head; I just heard them come out of my mouth. I said, "We've been in this growth conference, but I spell growth differently than these other men." I began to spell growth: G-R-O-W-U-P. Grow up. Mature. We don't need more people; we need mature people. I guarantee you it's tough to find a preacher today who would follow the admonition of Gideon. Most preachers would have a heart attack if God told them, "You have too many people."

All these pastors were looking at me, saying, "Tell us how to be a success." And I heard these words come out of my mouth, "I see only two things in the Bible that measure success: to be able to say, 'Father, of those you have given me, I have lost none,' (John 18:9) and to hear the words, 'Well done, good and faithful servant' (Matthew 25:21). That's success, whether you have five people or five million."

Did God give you the five or five million, or did advertising through Christian media give them to you? The doctrine of humanism gives way to preaching the latest doctrine of the day to tickle men's ears, being a respecter of persons, and fearing men's faces. That will help you add to your numbers. Did the doctrine of humanism give those people to you, or did God?

Chapter 2

Counterfeit Christianity

"Of them which thou gavest me have I lost none."
(John 18:9)

The disciples came to Jesus one day after He had taught a very hard thing, saying, "Master, you've offended the people!" Listen to the wisdom of Jesus' response: "Every plant, which my heavenly Father hath not planted, shall be rooted up." (Matthew 15:13) What God has plucked up, don't try to plant again. I believe much of what we are seeing today is God plucking out of churches, not planting into churches. He will add those that need to be added, but we need to get rid of some folks in order to have pure doctrine.

After Ananias and Sapphira were judged, "none of the rest [of that spirit] dared join them." (Acts 5:13 NKJV) You want to thin out your church? Have an Ananias and Sapphira experience. "Don't go down to that church and lie, or you'll drop dead!"

Much of the lying that is going on in our churches today is personal prophecy: "I have a word from the Lord for you, brother!" Often this is just lying, mimicking the Holy Ghost. I would to God that we would have a pure visitation and have our churches cleaned again. We could then rejoice in hearing, "Thus saith the Lord," knowing it was God who had spoken to us.

I question the behavior in some of the great meetings today where the power of God is seen. I was holding meetings years ago in which every person I'd touch would fall under the power. I got sick and tired of seeing people fall down. I'd see people looking back over their shoulders to see if someone was going to catch them. That is not the Holy Ghost. If it's the Holy Ghost, you don't need to catch them. God is not going to hurt anybody.

I noticed a man kneeling over a bench at the altar in front of the pews. I walked by and simply reached down and touched his forehead. He went up over his feet and under the front row. Now, that's the power of God! I'm tired of all this counterfeit, mocking the Holy Ghost.

We once held a meeting in a large auditorium with an orchestra pit. I lined everybody up against that pit, and not one person fell down. Before that, everybody fell down. Don't you want it to be God? Don't you want it to be the real thing? Then why are we selling out for all this show time, playing games? Paul said, "I've written this epistle to you that you might know how to behave yourself in the house of God." It's time to get back to the old paths. Turn off Christian television and open the pastoral epistles.

The fact of the matter is that Paul would not be welcome in many churches today, nor would Jesus. If Jesus were to come right now, what would you have to give Him, and what would it be built upon? Return to the old paths.

Jeremiah 2 speaks of two evils of that day: "They have forsaken me the fountain of living waters, and hewed them out cisterns, broken cisterns, that can hold no water." (Jeremiah 2:13) Do you know what those broken cisterns are today? Every man preaching what they hear their "brothers" preach. When was the last time you got your own message from God instead of teaching what you hear on Christian television? You are gambling with your salvation when you start taking all the bait that is out there. It may not have killed you yet, but it will.

We have denied the rivers of Living Water. We are drinking from men's cisterns, and our people are bound in covetousness and fear. We will stand before Him with blood dripping from our hands if we have loved our own reputation more than our flock.

Take heed to yourself and to your doctrine, that you might save both yourself and those who hear you. When you stand before Jesus, He's not going to be impressed with your Mercedes, and you won't need a Rolex watch in eternity. Who cares what time it is in eternity? You want me to tell you what time it is? Today is the day of salvation, that you might save both yourself and those who hear you.

Chapter 3
The Cost of the Old Paths

"For which of you, intending to build a tower, sitteth not down first, and counteth the cost, whether he have sufficient to finish it?" (Luke 14:28)

I'm going to share a principle with you that will make your church smaller. We reduced our church by about 70 percent. We had 70 percent of our church leave, yet our missions giving doubled, and we paid off all our property with Gideon's three hundred. If you'll preach and require the Word of the people that God wants you to have, He'll move you into the realm of the miraculous where you will no longer trust in the arm of the flesh. You either choose God, or you die! It's a good place to be!

It is so good to be free—free to say what God has for you to say, free from the fear of men's faces, free to be able to love people unconditionally. I've not run into many people like that. The process to get there hurts: you have to die. It is no longer I that live, but Christ that liveth in me. Are you willing to lose it all?

At the height of our popularity, God spoke the sixth chapter of Jeremiah to me. I had a multimillionaire say to me, "I will bankroll your ministry nationwide." Our Christian school was the fastest growing school in Washington, D.C. We were competing with the public schools in athletics, and preparing to build the largest sanctuary in the area. As I was in prayer, God spoke to me and said, "I'm not pleased with you. This is not what I called you to do." He took me to Jeremiah and said, "I'm giving you a decision right now:

choose the world's brand of success or the success that you spoke to those men in the church growth conference last year. Either hang out with the shakers and the movers or do what I called you to do."

Millions of dollars were put in my hands. I looked at that multimillionaire and said, "I'm not for sale. It won't be said that any man has made Abraham (or me) rich. I'm choosing the old paths."

I went back to the church and called together all the parents that had children in our school. Conversations with the parents went something like this: "Mr. and Mrs. Smith, God has spoken to us to go back to the old paths. Your son Johnny can come back to school next year, but Suzy cannot because she's too carnal. She loves the world and therefore is not welcome here."

As each family came in, I had to separate the sheep from the goats. Didn't parents get angry and leave? Yes, by the hundreds. Few there be that find it.

A few years ago, I had lunch with the pastor of a church that had just been built in Florida. The foyer of his church was like a luxurious hotel lobby. The church cost 20 million dollars at that time to build. As we were having lunch, tears flowed from his eyes. He said, "Star, what you're preaching is the truth, but that message won't pay the mortgage on this building. I have to tell the people what they want to hear."

Are you going to do what the Head of the church tells you to do or what your flesh tells you? Are you going to walk in faith or fear? Will you live for your glory or for His?

Chapter 4

Take Heed to Yourself

"Take heed unto thyself, and unto the doctrine;
continue in them: for in doing this thou shalt
both save thyself, and them that hear thee."
(1 Timothy 4:16)

Church growth starts with the pastor. Take heed to yourself. You have to deal with covetousness in your life before you can teach it to your people. "I'm not covetous; I'm not after more money." Maybe it's not money you're after but a reputation. Do you work hard so you can have the biggest church in your area? Do you hope to be on television someday? It's not just money we covet; we also covet fame and self-worth. Maybe you feel like you could do a better job if you had a hundred people instead of fifty. Would that be the sign that God has called and ordained you? But when you get two hundred people, you'll have to have two hundred and fifty people.

"How do I get more people?" Compromise the gospel, because few find this highway of holiness. Broad is the way that leads to destruction (Matthew 7:13). Those words were spoken to believers, people who thought they were right with God, not to the pagans. In essence, Jesus was saying, "There are too many people that think they are right. There is a straight and narrow path, but few find it" (verse 14).

Take heed to yourself and to your doctrine, for men will be covetous. Are you jealous of some of these men with big churches? "I preach as well as they do. I have a better education than they do. Why do they have that big church, and I have this small church? I heard that evangelist with all of those people sitting on the hillside. I preach as well as he does."

What does it matter what those other preachers are doing? What has God called you to do? Know who you are and what God has called you to do. Are you content, or do the spirits of covetousness, pride, and ambition drive you? If so, you will end up in false doctrine. In the last days, perilous times will come.

Chapter 5

Preach Paul's Doctrine

"Ever learning, and never able to come to the knowledge of the truth. Now as Jannes and Jambres withstood Moses, so do these also resist the truth: men of corrupt minds, reprobate concerning the faith." (2 Timothy 3:7-8)

Everybody runs to hear the prosperity teaching, but it isn't working for anybody except the guys teaching it. It doesn't work because it's not the truth; it's a false doctrine. Seek first the kingdom of God and His righteousness. Godliness with contentment is great gain.

"Perverse disputings of men of corrupt minds, and destitute of the truth, supposing that gain is godliness: from such withdraw thyself." (1 Timothy 6:5) The prosperity teachers tell us that if we are godly and are giving everything to God, we will be blessed and prosper. Isn't that the message? That's what I'm hearing them preach. I know these men. I have been on their airplanes, and I have been in their homes. They are deceived. I don't think they are evil people, but their doctrine is evil, even damnable. They think they are telling the truth, but Satan has blinded their eyes. "It must be God. Look at me! I've got all this stuff! Why isn't it working for others? Why doesn't it work for the people listening to me? Well, maybe there is sin in their lives. Maybe they are not as godly as I am." "From such withdraw yourself." If it doesn't work for everybody, it is not sound doctrine.

Paul tells Timothy, "Charge them that are rich in this world, that they be not highminded, nor trust in uncertain riches, but in the living God, who giveth us richly all things to enjoy; That they do good, that they be rich in good works, ready to distribute, willing to communicate." (1 Timothy 6:17-18) Now, why would Paul say "charge the rich" if everybody is supposed to be rich? What he is saying is that some of you are rich and some of you aren't. He didn't say some of you are godly and some of you aren't. It has nothing to do with godliness. It has to do with the sovereignty of God. Some people He chooses to make rich, and to some people He says, "I'll give you food and raiment; be content." Some people have big closets full of clothes, while others have only one change of clothes. This has nothing to do with how much faith they have or how godly they are, but whether God appointed them to that position or not. They are no better than the other people, no more spiritual, no more intelligent, and no more obedient. God puts us in the body as it pleases Him. Are you pleased with where God has put you, or did He make a mistake? Why were you born into this family, this tribe, this nation? Should you be prosperous in this nation? Has God made a mistake? Remember the doctrine of the apostle Paul by the Holy Spirit: "Godliness with contentment is great gain."

There are people who are "ever learning, and never able to come to the knowledge of the truth. But they shall proceed no further: for their folly shall be manifest unto all men." (2 Timothy 3:7, 9) I believe judgment is coming on America. I want to hear what these men preach when they lose all their stuff. I believe America is going to fall. America is Sodom and Gomorrah. America is the broken reed of Egypt. Do you remember the admonition of the prophet not to trust in that broken reed? Don't you trust in America; it is going down. Put your trust in God, because when America fails, God will not fail. He is the same God that can turn stones into bread. He can multiply the oil and the meal. He can send you ravens and pour manna out of heaven. Look to the hills from which comes your help (Psalm 121:1). Paul also says to the apostles, "But thou hast fully known my doctrine, manner of life, purpose, faith, longsuffering, charity, patience." (2 Timothy 3:10) Those around us are saying "peace and safety." If you are godly, you won't have any problems," I want you to hear this: "Yea, and all that will live godly in Christ Jesus shall suffer persecution." (verse 12)

Paul says, "You have known my hard afflictions. You have heard of my shipwrecks, my beatings. My own people hate me. I have endured, and the Lord delivered me out of them all." The doctrine of prosperity says there are no problems; my doctrine says there are many, but God will deliver you out of them all. Don't count it a strange thing when you see yourself in the fiery trials, the apostle says. They are common to all of us as believers. God will not try you past that which you are able to stand. With every temptation, He makes the way of escape (1 Corinthians 10:13). Wherever you are today—in a place of pressure or fire—allow God to purify your life at this moment.

Times of prosperity are dangerous, but it's very safe in trial and affliction. In these times of trial, all the weights and sins that so easily beset us are burned off, and all of our ambition is put aside. Then, if God chooses to do something different with our lives, the blessings of the Lord make rich and add no sorrow. Blessings that are not of God will add sorrow; they will kill you. The cares of the world will choke the Word of God out of your life. But when God blesses, there is no sorrow. You are not afraid of losing the blessing, you are not afraid to distribute it, nor do you believe that you got it by yourself. God said to be very careful when you go into the Promised Land lest you say, "Look what I got by my own righteousness and by my own strength," and you forget the Lord. This is the doctrine of Paul. Are you preaching Pauline doctrine or the doctrine heard on Christian television?

Chapter 6

A Blameless Steward

"For a bishop must be blameless, as the steward of God." (Titus 1:7)

L et's find out if you are even qualified, if you are truly apostles, prophets, evangelists, pastors, or teachers. First, ask yourself, "Is perfection the standard of my ministry?" Second, "Is my life blameless?" "A bishop then must be blameless." (1 Timothy 3:2) To be blameless doesn't mean we never sin or never do anything wrong. If that were the case, we would all have to quit right now, and I would be the first one out the door.

To be blameless means that no one can lay hold of you. There is nothing hidden in your life that would bring a reproach to the gospel. You pay your bills on time. Your word is your bond. When you say you are going to be somewhere at nine o'clock but encounter a traffic jam along the way preventing you from making it on time, that is one thing. But when you say you are going to be there at nine o'clock yet have no intention of being there at nine, that is another matter. You are no longer blameless, because your word doesn't mean anything. When you say you are going to pay someone on a certain day yet don't pay because an emergency arose, that is one thing. But if you had no intention of paying on that day and were just trying to get the person out of your face, that is altogether a different matter.

Scripture says that we are to be spoken well of by those who are within and without. We know the world will hate us and try to bring a reproach upon us, but they will have no facts, evidence, or proof to back up their statements. This is what it means to be blameless: there is no proof for their accusations.

Chapter 7

A Temperate Life

"If any be blameless, the husband of one wife, having faithful children not accused of riot or unruly. For a bishop must be blameless, as the steward of God… temperate; Holding fast the faithful word as he hath been taught…" (Titus 1:6-9)

Are you living a blameless life as it concerns your children and your wife? Some of you are running from meeting to meeting, ignoring your children. One thing that grieves my heart as I look at the church is the youth. Where are the children that have a heart for God? Where is the love within the family that is representative of the union of the church of Jesus Christ? The local church can never be stronger than the individual families of which it is made. If you are a man of God, you will be building strong homes, for they are what make strong churches.

Paul then writes that the bishop must be "the husband of one wife." This is not a reference to polygamy, but speaks of a man who loves his wife as Christ loves the church and gives himself for it. The Greek rendering literally means a "one-woman man." As the body sees you loving your wife, they will see you as a man capable of loving them. The church will see a tenderness and care, and they'll know you are going to care for them. They will also see you as the head, the authority over your wife, and they'll know that you will be the authority over them. You will not abdicate your responsibility, nor will you look outside your wife for any other strength or comfort.

Often, women like to come up to the preacher and tell him how great he is. "Oh, Pastor, you are such a great man of God. I wish my husband were as spiritual as you." Do not entertain that flattery for a moment. I don't need to hear that from any woman but my wife. I don't need my ego stroked by anybody other than my wife. Her job is to tell me how great I am, even when I'm not. My wife tells me how handsome I am. I have a mirror; I know what I look like! But that's her job: she is fulfilling her role to me as the church fulfills its role to Jesus.

One of the most dangerous things to your ministry is a woman who will try to bring you down. Never counsel a woman alone. Always have another pastor, deacon, or your wife with you. Don't be seduced by the flattery of other women. When the church sees you being faithful to your wife, they know you will be faithful to them.

The man of God is to be vigilant, meaning, "to be sober; temperate." You have control of your life. You are not given to excessive sleep or labor. You don't have to run to every meeting, but maintain a proper balance between home and ministry. Jesus gave us power to be witnesses, to lay hands on the sick, to cast out devils, and to raise the dead. Programs founded in worldly wisdom won't do that. They don't cast out devils; they send them to psychiatrists. They don't lay hands on the sick; they send them to doctors. There is a wisdom and power available to us, but we must sanctify ourselves to carry this glory. We must strip off the kingly robes to take on the priestly ephod.

Chapter 8

Proven Faithful

"But we have this treasure in earthen vessels, that the excellency of the power may be of God, and not of us." (2 Corinthians 4:7)

Next, we see that men of God cannot be novices. 1 Timothy 3:10 says, "And let these also first be proved; then let them use the office of a deacon." A novice is one who is inexperienced. It is possible for a young man to be supernaturally mature, so this word is not referring to time but to maturity. A person may have been a Christian for 20 years yet still be a novice, or may have been a Christian for 20 weeks yet be mature. What must be determined is the working of God's grace and gifts in the individual. His life has to be proven faithful to the kingdom of God.

How do we know if we have made the right decision in placing a man into the office of bishop? If he is placed improperly, he will be lifted up with pride: "Not a novice, lest being lifted up with pride he fall into condemnation of the devil." (verse 6) Are you proud of your call and your position in the body of Christ as a minister? Then get out; you are a novice. What is there to boast in? We are just unprofitable servants and are only doing what has been required of us. Everything we have, we have received of God. The glory and the excellency is of God, not of us. We are just earthen vessels through which the anointing flows.

It is easy to recognize a novice. He struts around like he is something, expecting people to bow to him as the man of God.

It doesn't matter how long he has been in the ministry. If that spirit is in him, he doesn't belong there. Too many people are in the ministry for their own glory.

Some time ago, a young man came to me from Rhema Bible Institute in Oklahoma, saying, "Brother Scott, I would like to labor with you in the ministry. I'm an apostle."

I asked, "Who told you that?"

"Well, the Lord told me."

Where is the evidence? What makes a person an apostle? I won't elaborate on all the credentials passed out by Rhema Bible College, but everyone who graduated from there had to have a title: "I'm an apostle…I'm a prophet'…I'm an evangelist."

No, you are carnal if you are seeking titles instead of ministry. Your gift will make room for you. Your fruit will tell what you are, not what you put on your business card.

Chapter 9

Rule Your House Well

"A bishop then must be blameless, the husband of one wife, vigilant, sober...no striker...One that ruleth well his own house..." (1 Timothy 3:2-4)

How vigilant are you when it comes to caring for your family? The word vigilant also means to be "dispassionate; calm." Are you calm? Can you stay laid back in the ministry when everything around you is going crazy? To be vigilant is to remain dispassionate: there is no fear in your household, nor are you an angry man. The congregation can see how peaceful your family is, which ministers peace to the flock. They will be as calm as you are in the time of adversity. It is important for leadership to remain peaceful, trusting in the leadership of Jesus.

The word that follows, sober, speaks of "earnestness or sincerity." People will know if you are trying to use them for your own purposes. They will know the sincerity of your heart by how you reflect the love of God to your family.

Scripture says that we are to not be a "striker" (verse 3). This is one who retaliates, who is hostile. You will never be a striker if you are in authority at all times. You don't have to strike anyone if you know you are in authority, in charge, and your word is truth. You just look your wife in the eye and say, "As for me and my house, we are serving God. If you are not going to submit, I am putting you out. I am not going to hit you; I am just going to put you away."

Most men will not do that, because they want someone to cook their meals and to have sex with—total selfishness rather than love. They refuse to take authority because of what it will cost them. They love themselves more than they love their wives or children. That is exactly why Adam partook of that fruit in the first place. He chose Eve over God.

My wife and my children know they are not first in my life. I am going to serve the Lord first, and only then can I love them properly and require righteousness of them.

If you cannot rule your family, get out of the ministry. Sit in the local church and be fitly joined together and perfected by the rest of the saints. If God is for you, as He was for David, He will send you back to be king. If not, the will of the Lord be done. That would be some of the greatest leadership you ever showed your family. If you want to show your family your seriousness for the kingdom, demand order by telling the rebellious to get out. Either way, they will see you are serious about serving God.

To desire the office of a bishop is to desire a good work. You must rule your house well and have your children in subjection with all gravity. The children don't have to be born again, but they have to be under control. "For if a man know not how to rule his own house, how shall he take care of the church of God?" (I Timothy 3:4)

Chapter 10

Children Jealous for God's Glory

"A bishop then must be…One that ruleth well his own house, having his children in subjection with all gravity…" (1 Timothy 3:2-4)

When my children were younger, I was very busy traveling and ministering outside the church. I would be home almost every Sunday, but throughout the week I was ministering in many other places. I was busy recording live television and radio programs, and teaching in Full Gospel Business Men's meetings and rallies. I was rarely at home, but my family was always with me. My life was temperate—organized and in control.

Preaching is not more important than your family. What does it profit you to gain the world and lose your own children? Don't allow them to resent the ministry; make them part of it. When my son was only five years old, I would leave the meeting and go out to the tape table, and see his little eyes just above the level of the table. He was serving Jesus, laboring with Dad. He took the money and gave away the tapes. He grew up as a part of the ministry, not resenting it.

We are to create a jealousy for God's glory in our children. We are not to raise a mingled seed, but a godly seed who will rise up and call us blessed. What will remain after we are gone, when our ministry is over? I am not building for my own glory and ease, but trying to leave something. If Jesus tarries, I want people to be here who will continue to preach the gospel. God chose Abraham because he would teach his children and his children's children.

The apostle Paul wrote that our children must be "in subjection with all gravity." The word gravity, meaning, "with seriousness; dignity," is very important. Are your children serious about God? Have you trained them in the fear of the Lord? Remember what happened in the community of believers in the Old Testament. When a child was rebellious, he was taken to the city gates and stoned to death, and the parents threw the first stone! Are your children aware of the consequence to their rebellion and their disorder in the home? Today, we don't physically kill the child, but we can turn him over to Satan for the destruction of his flesh. We can tell our children that if they want to live like the world—the pagans—we will send them to some of their relatives who are pagans. "You don't want to worship the Lord? Then go live with people who worship the devil. But as for me and my house, we are serving God."

If you cannot do that, get out of the ministry. There is no biblical requirement that your children be born again in order for you to be used in ministry. You cannot make anybody get saved, but there is a requirement that they be obedient and orderly. They must know how to behave themselves in the house of God. What cost Eli his ministry? "Nay, nay, my son," he said to his sons who were drunken, disorderly, and lying with women in the church. You have to be willing to overlook your natural children and pour your heart into the "Samuels" among you, because true family are those who are of the household of faith.

Your children should know this commitment you have to the kingdom. 'in a rebellious manner, I had only two choices. I would either put them out, or I would get out of the ministry. As for me and my house, we would serve God. They would have to find another home if they didn't want to serve the Lord.

Chapter 11

The Word Sanctifies

"Sanctify them through thy truth: thy word is truth."
(John 17:17)

If we are to be shepherds after God's own heart, we must bring people into green pastures and cause them to drink deeply from the still waters. "Study to show thyself approved unto God, a workman that needeth not to be ashamed, rightly dividing the Word of truth." (2 Timothy 2:15) To rightly divide the Word of truth is to cut straight through it. We preachers use too many words; we need to cut straight through to the truth. We don't have to give an explanation for everything we say. The spiritual mind discerns the things of the Spirit, and we will never convince the carnal mind anyway. We spend too many of our words trying to convince the carnal mind to believe. The truth is spiritually discerned.

Study to show yourselves approved of God by using the methods of God. The Spirit is the teacher; we are the earthen vessels through which the glory of God flows. Many of us depend upon our eloquence, our personalities, or our fervency, and mistake those things for anointing. The real glory is seen when we become earthen vessels, and the glory of God that flows through us gets the attention.

If we speak the Word He has spoken to us, then it is anointed. We sometimes try to add to the Word of God because we don't believe it. We are not confident in its own power, so we have to add something to convince people. This Word is like a hammer, which will break the rock into pieces. It will breakthe hardest heart. Without our human effort, it will be a fire in our mouths that consumes those before us. This is what it means to show ourselves approved unto God, rightly applying the Word of God. Let the Word and its truth defend itself.

As preachers, never forget that we always step up to the Word of God. There is nothing higher or more important in our services than bringing forth the truth of God's Word. It is the truth of the Word that sets us free.

Chapter 12

One Church, One Lord

"For the perfecting of the saints, for the work of the ministry, for the edifying of the body of Christ:" (Ephesians 4:12)

The pastor's job is to perfect the saints, and the standard for your ministry can be none other than perfection. I am not referring to the false doctrine of sinless perfection, which claims that after you have received the second work of grace you are sanctified and never sin anymore. What kind of perfection am I talking about? The word perfect means "to mature, to bring to its complete end." And the "end" is "when he shall appear, we shall be like him." (1 John 3:2) Our standard is not perfect performance, but perfect pursuit.

I don't know about you, but I don't always get it right. How many of you have sinned in the last year? You don't always get it right, but is your pursuit perfect? Do you hunger for holiness like the hart pants for the brook? Are you more jealous for God's glory than for your own reputation?

I told you that 100 percent of our members tithe. Why is that? It's because I won't allow anything else. Are they all so spiritual that they are never tempted to keep some of the money for themselves? No, they have the same temptations that I do, that you do, and that the people in your congregation do, but there is a standard. They can't rob from God and be a part of my congregation. They can't be a thief, stealing God's glory, and then come and lift their hands, pretending to worship Him in our services.

What is the standard in your church? Can you have a different doctrine than I have? There is only one church, one body, one faith, one Lord. What are you doing about it? "Well, if I do that, people are going to leave. I would rather put their five percent in my pocket than nothing. I would rather have their crumbs than nothing to put in my pocket." So, it's about you, and not the glory of God? Then you have no business being a shepherd.

In our congregation, all of our members attend every service. We have the same attendance Sunday morning, Sunday night, and Wednesday night. Why? It's because I don't allow anything else. "But we are busy." If you are too busy for church, then you are too busy. You find something else to cut out, but you are not cutting out church. We are "not forsaking the assembling of ourselves together, as the manner of some is; but exhorting one another: and so much the more, as we see the day approaching." (Hebrews 10:25)

Is that day approaching? Do you believe that Jesus is coming back? Then why are you not requiring your people to come to church? "I can't make them come to church." No, but you can send them to another church. Let them know if they are not attending regularly to go somewhere else. If they are to be members here, they are to come, because the standard is perfection.

Our job is to perfect the saints to do the work of the ministry.

Chapter 13

Body Ministry Through Unification

"And he gave some, apostles; and some, prophets; and some, evangelists; and some, pastors and teachers; For the perfecting of the saints, for the work of the ministry, for the edifying of the body of Christ:" (Ephesians 4:11-12)

The saints do the work of the ministry. If you truly want to minister for God, then stay in the local church and be perfected, and you will do the ministry. The ministry doesn't come from the preacher but from the body. True ministry is in the body, not the head.

The great mystery of godliness is in the new creation, the transformation of mind and heart. This is made evident by a love of the brethren and pouring out our lives into building the church rather than our own personal kingdoms. The world will be able to observe and say, "Behold, how they love one another!" This is why the local church is so important.

The Scripture says when they see this mature love, the world cannot deny that God has raised Jesus from the dead. What we read in the fourth chapter of Ephesians is supernatural. Our natural tendency is for each of us to do our own thing, but as spiritual leaders, we must require unification of the body of Christ. If you are truly called of God, you will perfect the saints to do the work of the ministry. There will be no other standard but perfection in your ministry, and your emphasis will be on unifying the body, causing people to "grow up into Him." (Ephesians 4:15)

How does maturation occur? It would be impossible to sit down with every member and pour your life into them. You need to make disciples. Surround yourself with a core of believers like Jesus did, and then let them begin to multiply as they become "fitly joined together." (verse 16) The Greek meaning for the phrase fitly joined together is to "bring proper organization." Is your ministry organized? Do you have a plan? Does everyone know his or her place in the body of Christ, or is each one just following "the leading of the Lord"? The head of the church, Jesus, has placed ministry gifts in the body as it pleases Him, and we, ministry gifts operating as His representatives, place the members in the local church for the good of the community.

"Pastor, I really feel called to lead worship and be one of the worship leaders."

"What we need is someone to clean the toilets. Give me that microphone and take this mop!"

How many people are called to the mop ministry? Everybody wants a microphone, a title, to be the greatest among us, but a servant's heart is what is really needed. It is your job to bring that spirit. Don't be tempted to bow down to their desires and try to make room for certain gifts that come to your ministry. If someone comes who can play the keyboard better than any you have ever heard, but you don't know him, first let him know, "Here's the mop...Prove yourself...Be knit in...Learn to serve...Follow the proper organization." Perhaps they just want to come and bless your people and be a part of your ministry, but we lay hands on no man suddenly.

Chapter 14

Uphold the Standard

"But I keep under my body, and bring it into subjection: lest that by any means, when I have preached to others, I myself should be a castaway." (1 Corinthians 9:27)

It is always difficult to talk to preachers because they think they already know everything. "I can hear from God. I'm the man of God. I know that Scripture." Are you living by it? You don't really know the Scriptures if they are not dominating your life. A parrot can be taught to quote a verse. Most preachers are parrots, just preaching what they have heard somebody else preach. Has the coal been taken from the altar and put upon your lips? Have you encountered the glory of God, or are you nothing more than a hireling, preaching for filthy lucre just to get a little food for your mouth?

We will learn how to get the strength to become doers of the Word and not hearers only, deceiving ourselves. Many of us can quote the Word, but we're not living the Word. We preach to others, but we become castaways. We learned the need for taking heed to ourselves and to our doctrine, that we might save both ourselves and those that hear us (1 Timothy 4:16). Isn't it interesting that the apostle was concerned about Timothy's salvation? It is easy to lose our salvation in the ministry. Who is it that Satan is trying to destroy but the leaders?

Have you ever truly repented before your congregation? I don't mean saying you are sorry, but revealing sin, and changing.

Repentance does not mean, "I am sorry; this is what I did." True repentance says, "What I did was sin, and I am changing and going in this direction." Godly sorrow is never repented of; just stay on course. Tell the people, "You know my manner of life, and you know my purpose. I was teaching this doctrine because I wanted to be more popular; I wanted recognition among the other preachers; I wanted to be a success. But I have received the spirit of truth and have come to realize that I am just an under shepherd. Here is what I am going to do to become more like the Chief Shepherd of our souls." Then speak the truth to them.

Defend the doctrine, not your performance. Keep perfection as the standard. Humble yourself: be willing to confess your sin, and let your people know that you are just a man, an earthen vessel. Let them know that the glory coming out of you is the truth of God's Word and that it won't change for you, nor will it change for them. If you don't fall upon the rock and become broken, it will fall on you and grind you to powder (Luke 20:18). Hold the standard of perfection before your congregation.

Chapter 15

Make Strong Disciples

"From whom the whole body fitly joined together and compacted by that which every joint supplieth... maketh increase of the body unto the edifying of itself in love." (Ephesians 4:16)

The most important ministry is not outside the body but in the body, maturing and building people to become a church that edifies itself in love. We often leave all the weak people in the church, and send all the strong people out preaching. Evangelism is not the most important purpose of the church; discipleship is. It is not enough just to go into all the world and preach the gospel. Once people come into the kingdom, they must be perfected. The mortality rate in the church is horrendous.

The phrase fitly joined means "to frame up properly." In any construction, you know how important it is to set the cornerstone plumb. The good thing about the Church is that the Cornerstone—Jesus—is perfect, so everything in your ministry has to be built in direct correlation to the Cornerstone. The admonition is to "take heed how you build" (1 Corinthians 3:10). How dare we, as men of God, just shoddily throw something on this foundation so that we can get on to another project, or so that people can see who we are. Take the time necessary to build a sure, perfect ministry.

Make sure you don't go on to your next project until you see a strong body, knit together, able to care for itself, so that they are not tossed to-and-fro by every wind of doctrine. Then when these national speakers—reeds blowing in the wind—come to town, your people are not seduced to run to them. "Why should I go hear this great name? All of my needs are being met at home. I have a pastor who feeds me, and brothers and sisters interwoven in my life who nourish me. The big-name preacher won't come and lift up my hands when they are hanging down, but this brother who has been knit into my life will. The big-name preacher won't weep when my child dies, but that member who has been knit together with me will lift me up in prayer. He will weep when I weep and rejoice when I rejoice." That is the strength of the body of Christ.

Instead, we have people running to and fro to every new thing that is coming down the pike. The people in our congregation don't run to hear the big shot in town, because they have been edified in love. Why would they go to hear these people if it were not for a lack in their lives? They may think there is some special gift that will be imparted to them if you are not doing your job, if your people are not fed and nourished and loved.

"But I am supporting that man when he comes so that I will be able to sit on the platform and everybody will see me. This will help advertise my ministry, and people will know that I am a man called of God." The good shepherd lays down his life for the sheep. Instead of sitting on the platform of the big meeting, you should be at home, praying to minister to your own people.

"From whom the whole body fitly joined together and compacted by 'compacted, a powerful word and one of the most important things we will address. How easily can your ministry be torn apart? What tendency is there for your flock to run to this or that preacher? The word compacted in the Greek means "to be united or knit together," like a rope that is bound. Don't keep your people dependent upon you. Cause them to look to one another for strength and edification. Let their lives become so intertwined that they know who is there for them. Then you will have done the work of God.

Chapter 16

Follow Me as I Follow Christ

"But thou hast fully known my doctrine, manner of life, purpose…" (2 Timothy 3:10)

Does your flock know your purpose? Do you know your purpose? Are you sure of what you are supposed to be doing right now? Hopefully, you have a word from the Lord, and you know what He has told you to do. If you don't know where you are going, the flock will be uncomfortable.

It is important for your flock to get to know you. Too many people think we preachers are supposed to stay apart and separate because we are so holy, when, in fact, we are the servants of all. That does not mean we do the work for the people, but, in fact, our primary calling is to instruct them and perfect them to do the work of the ministry. They will never become more mature or perfect than when we let them get close to us and see our maturity.

Paul told Timothy to "stir up the gift of God, which is in thee by the putting on of my hands." (2 Timothy 1:6) Timothy did not get the doctrine by hearing Paul teach, but through the intimacy of imbibing his spirit. Let the people get close to you and know your heart; then you can look at them and say, "Follow me as I follow Christ" (Hebrews 13:7, Philippians 3:12).

When your people know you are not trying to put forth your will but sharing the will of God, they will follow, because His sheep know His voice, and another they will not follow (John 10:14, 5).

Your main job as a preacher is to get rid of your voice and let the voice of God be heard. Your people are not stupid; they know the difference between your projects and God's kingdom. When you say they are rebellious, you are just saying that they won't do your will, when, in fact, you are the rebel. They are only trying to follow the Chief Shepherd. Don't beat your sheep because they will not do your will. They just want to obey their Father, and they can tell the difference, because another they will not follow.

Your main job as pastor is to bring strength to your congregation. Many of you leave your people weak so that you can look strong. Many of you are afraid that if your people get too spiritual, they will take over the church. Did God call you or not?

Build up your people into the image of Jesus by building your people beyond yourself. Many of us are intimidated by talents and gifts that come into our church. Don't be intimidated; God sent them to you. If God called you, He will defend you if they turn against you. Just be like David in sending the ark back to the city and say, "If God wants me to return, then I'll return." (2 Samuel 15:25 26)

Chapter 17

Perfect the Saints

"This poor widow hath cast more in, than all they which have cast into the treasury: For all they did cast in of their abundance; but she of her want did cast in all that she had, even all her living." (Mark 12:42-44)

I was told that a well-known preacher from Mombasa recently said that if you could not give 2,000 shillings in his offering, then you were not a true pastor. That's a blasphemous statement! Jesus said that the widow who gave two mites gave more than everybody else put together. Who does this man think he is, to set a different standard than Jesus did?

I have a question for you: What if, just as I was walking into that meeting, the Holy Spirit spoke to me, saying, "Give that person all your money?" I no longer have 2,000 shillings to line the preacher's pocket, and although he said I wasn't a preacher, I perfectly fulfilled the law of giving.

God set up the church to operate from the tithe and the offerings. Men, like this guy who said to give 2,000 shillings, do that because they have built beyond their faith. Their ministries have grown bigger than God's method to support them, so they have to use man's methods. God will always support what He has called you to do. If your faith and God's methods don't support it, God is not in it. Go back to Bethel, where you last heard from God, and find out what God is telling you to do. It's easy to get confused and distracted by these other men who are preaching this nonsense. You see their kingdoms and are in awe. Go back to Bethel and find out what God said to you. What is the last thing He said? I don't know exactly, but I do know He told you this: Perfect the saints.

Do your people tithe? You may think, "We live out in the country where the people are too poor to tithe." How can you be too poor to tithe? What is the tithe? It is ten percent. If you have nothing, ten percent of nothing is what? Nothing. So teach your people to tithe nothing. Have them put nothing in the offering to the glory of God. "Father, I thank You that this week You have given me nothing; in direct accordance with how You have blessed me, I worship You. Amen."

The one who has a dollar puts in a dime. "But he has only a dollar!" That's alright. Ten percent is a dime. "But he will have only 90 cents left!" To hold back the extra ten percent is not going to make a difference anyway, but it will bring a curse on him. To give it in faith will bring the blessings of God.

"Do you mean he will be rich?" I did not say that. I said "the blessings," however God chooses to bless. The key is in honoring God. I am not interested in the money our people are giving. I am interested in them glorifying God, because a day may come when they will have no money to give, but we can still come together and glorify God. We now have an environment in which the miraculous can take place, in which God can come in and supernaturally sustain us. That is why we perfect the saints.

Not many people are doing the Word of God today. You may think I'm strange, but I won't change for you or anybody else. This thing works. I would rather have 30 people who are serious than 3,000 who are parasites; because when it's over, I'll have something to give to God, but those 3,000 will have gone to a devil's hell. If I don't do what the Word of God says, I'll have no riches in heaven, and their blood will drip from my hands. I want people to like me, but I would rather hear, "Well done, thou good and faithful servant" (Matthew 25:21).

Are you called of God, or not?

Chapter 18

Be a Pattern for the Flock

"Neither as being lords over God's heritage, but
being ensamples to the flock." (1 Peter 5:3)

L isten to the admonition: "Feed the flock of God." (1 Peter 5:2)
The Greek word for "feed" is *poimaino*, which means "to lead
and nourish." Many of us want to lead. We say, "Follow us; we're the
shepherds," but we don't nourish the flock with the Word to make
them strong enough to follow.

"Feed the flock of God which is among you, taking the oversight
thereof." This means we are to grasp leadership. We don't look
to the flock for direction. We don't ask them what they think is
best for them, but we lead them to the still waters and into the
green pastures as our Shepherd leads us. Do you know where the
refreshing is? Do you know how to refresh a spirit in the anointing
of God? The Scripture says it is by reason of use, exercise (Hebrews
5:14). We become stronger by exercise—by doing the Word of God.
Are you looking for ways to become stronger, or are you content
with your spiritual condition?

"[Take] the oversight…Neither as being lords over God's heritage,
but being ensamples to the flock." Being an ensample means "to be
a pattern." People ought to look at our lives and say, "That's what
I want to be." Do the members of your church want to be just like
you? Do the young people in your church want to be just like you?
This is what it means to be a pattern—an example of the believer in

word and in truth and in all manner of our living.

Feed the flock of God. Do not be lords over God's heritage. Your congregation is God's heritage. Your role as minister is to be an example, a pattern, to the flock. We should be reproducing ourselves in our congregation. We should be able to tell them, "Follow me as I follow Christ."

Most of us only want our congregations to listen to our doctrine, rather than laying our lives down as patterns. As Americans, we heard from our parents, "Don't do as I do; do as I say." "Don't smoke; it's not good for you," but our parents smoked. "Don't drink," but they drank. That's what my father told me, but he smoked and drank. Consequently, I did what he did, not what he said. Be a pattern to your flock.

Chapter 19

Guard Against Covetousness

"For from the least of them even unto the greatest of them every one is given to covetousness; and from the prophet even unto the priest every one dealeth falsely." (Jeremiah 6:13)

This is the message we're hearing today: "You're alright. God accepts you like you are. Don't worry about this doctrine of holiness. God's merciful." He is! But He's also just. Too many people today are being destroyed by covetousness and lust, and being told that these are the blessings of God.

Are you ready to hear what the Spirit of God has to say to us, even if it goes contrary to today's fads, even if you may not get a gold watch or drive a Mercedes? The message you're hearing in professed Christendom is false doctrine. The apostle Paul said to withdraw from those who suppose that gain is godliness (1 Timothy 6:5). Gain is not wrong; it simply doesn't correspond directly with godliness. You can't tell how spiritual somebody is by what he possesses, and not everyone who gives can believe for a hundredfold return.

Only one person in the Bible was ever promised a hundredfold return (Mark 10:30). He was a person who forsook everything. He didn't put in a dollar and get a hundred back. Put it all in! Put your life in, and then He gives you a hundredfold in this life, and in the life to come, eternal life. You may not get a hundredfold now, but the promise is, "Seek ye first the kingdom of God, and his righteousness; and all these things shall be added unto you."

(Matthew 6:33) Stop seeking a hundredfold and start seeking the kingdom and righteousness, and then God's blessings will overtake you. What path are you on today?

I've been with preachers on their private planes and yachts, and I have a question. Why does this doctrine work only for the preachers? How come no one is getting rich except the preachers? "Just keep giving; God will bless you with a hundredfold return. Give into this ministry and God will bless you!" But they're the only ones getting blessed. I've heard their testimonies about how they gave a plane away and God gave them another one. They gave their plane to their best friend and their friend gave them a plane, and they are so blessed! Why didn't they give you the plane?

Choose the old paths. The Scripture says there is no lion to devour you on the highway of holiness (Isaiah 35:8-9). I live prosperity; I don't preach it. God has blessed me. I've never asked anybody for a dime in my life. I've never asked for a penny to go preach the gospel. I could name some preachers you would know who wanted to come and preach in our church a number of years ago. I think the reason was they heard that our people give. Some of them wanted us to sign a contract saying we would pick them up at the airport in a Rolls Royce. They wanted a guaranteed $20,000 offering. I told them to stay home. We need shepherds, not hirelings.

Why are so many people being deceived by a "new" path—this doctrine of covetousness? Because it's in every one of us; we all have that same sin in our flesh. Aren't you glad for the greater One who lives in us and keeps covetousness from dominating our lives? Since we know it's there, we need to guard against it and protect our people from it.

The Holy Pastor

Chapter 20

Presiding Well Over
Your Own Home

"One that ruleth well his own house, having his children in subjection with all gravity." (1 Timothy 3:4)

This passage of Scripture is so important to what God has called us to do in ruling our own homes. This word "rule" means "to preside over, to superintend, to stand before, to lead, to feed." "Oh, you mean I'm not just pastor at church; I'm also pastor of the home?" That's what it says. When it talks about ruling our homes well, it's talking very clearly about our pastoral responsibilities to the home first.

What he's saying to us very clearly is that if you can't pastor your home, you can't pastor the church. I'm going to say it again a different way. If you will not assume the pastoral care of your home, which is the first requirement, how can you say that God is calling you here or there, or to preach the gospel, or to run and do this or that? The first requirement for going to preach is pastoring your home first. Do you want me to tell you when you can go preach? You can go preach when you love your wife and lay your life down for her as Christ loved the church.

We talk about your role as overseer in your home because if you can't rule your home, you have no business overseeing the church of Jesus Christ. Some of you just let that comment go right by. I'm telling you, God is not going to wink at it. He will never bless you when you reject Him, despise His Word, and lower His standards. We said the other day that the first requirement of the bishop, the man of God, the elder, is humility. Humility: God is right, not me.

Chapter 21

Homes Totally out of Order

"Let every soul be subject unto the higher powers.
For there is no power but of God: the powers that
be are ordained of God. Whosoever therefore
resisteth the power, resisteth the ordinance of God."
(Romans 13:1-2)

It's humorous to me to go to some of these countries we've ministered in, like Kenya and St. Kitts, that are more blatantly matriarchal than our society, that refuse to see the distinction that God has made between men and women and their roles of authority and responsibility.

A number of people in a particular fellowship, having come out of different backgrounds, church affiliations, and perceived religious organizations, wanted the pastor to be accountable to them. They wanted him to tell them why, when, and how come. We talked with them just a little bit. I asked them, "Is that how you operate your household? Does your home operate that way? Do you answer to your wife and children?" They said, "Yes." That explained part of the problem. No, they didn't actually verbalize that. They just do it; they live it with homes totally out of order, no authority, each person an entity to himself.

Do you operate that way in your home? When you say it's time for bed, do your children say, "I'll pray about it, Daddy. No, I don't feel the Lord's leading me to bed at this moment."? The authority doesn't bear the sword in vain, Romans 13 tells us. God is going to back the authority. To resist the power is to resist God. It's rebellion; it's confusion. Every evil work begins to move in that kind of an environment.

Chapter 22

Keeping the Standards at Home

"If any be blameless, the husband of one wife, having faithful children not accused of riot or unruly." (Titus 1:6)

We see that it talks about children also, faithful children. Interesting word, that word "faithful." It's *pistos* in the Greek, meaning "believing." It's talking about saved kids. When it talks about our children being "saved" and "not accused of riot," the word "riot," in the Greek *asotia*, really talks about "an abandoned mind or life." It really means "unsaved." They can't have a life contrary to the Word of God. "Oh, so they're to be saved?" Yes. "What if my children are not born again? Can I still be a preacher?" Yes, if their life is not "a riot," if they're not out of control, if they're "pleased to dwell," like the unsaved husband or wife in this home that you're pastoring. If you're keeping the standards at home, you can then oversee the church.

You can't make people get saved. You can't make your wife get saved. You can't make your children get saved. Keep the gospel pure and the standards holy—those that won't live by them have to go somewhere else—if you want to preach the gospel. If you want to keep them there, then get out of the ministry; but don't think you can keep your home disorderly and then rule the house of God and set it in order. If you allow unsaved children in your home to riot or cause confusion, if you have a rebellious wife, then you're going to have a rebellious church. If you'll allow them in your home, you'll let them in your church. I didn't make up the rules; I'm just reading them to you. It's very important, beloved.

You see the terms "riot" and "unruly." "Unruly" means "not subject to your authority," or "out of control." Can I ask you something? Are your children under your control? They don't have to be born again or regenerated. Are they under your control, or are they bringing a reproach on your home? They may not be saved, but do they obey? Are they disciplined? Are they doing what you require them to do? You may not know what they're doing behind your back. You can't do anything about that unless God exposes it, but that's the requirement.

Chapter 23

Involved in the Lives of Your Children

"One that ruleth well his own house, having his children in subjection with all gravity." (1 Timothy 3:4)

When it talks about the importance of ruling our own homes well and having our children in subjection with all gravity, that word "gravity" means "to be serious, sober" about the responsibility you have as a father to your children. You are first to be involved in the lives of your children and see that they're born again. You're to train up your children in the nurture and the admonition of the Lord so that when they're old, they will not depart from it. The father is to train the child, to bring into his mind the biblical principles and then require them to be lived.

How dare we run around the streets of Nairobi or the countryside of Kenya preaching the gospel when we haven't taken time to sit with our own children, to love them, and to teach them the Word! Do you know what your kids ought to hear you say every once in a while when somebody asks, "Brother, can you come and preach for us?" Your children ought to hear you say, "No, I can't preach. I'm going to spend time with my son." "You mean I'm to put my son before the ministry?" Your son is the ministry; your daughter is the ministry; your wife is the ministry. "Yeah, but if I don't go preach there, maybe souls will go to hell!" God will send somebody else. He'll send the guy who spent time with his son last week! Do you know that the world can get by without you being too busy every day and every week to minister in your home? When you stand before Jesus, you won't have any blood on your hands.

Do you want to know one good way to do things? The way I used to do it was to take my kids with me. I involved them in the ministry. My daughter would sing when she was only twelve years old. My son would take care of tapes and sell books. He was barely big enough to see over the table, but he'd be handing people tapes. Make them a part of what you're doing so that they don't resent the ministry; they're part of the ministry. Let them understand how important their lives are, and then you won't end up like Eli, with children fornicating in the temple because you had no control over them.

We begin to see how awesome this responsibility is. If you can't rule your home (if your wife is not submissive, if your children are not obedient, if you're not loving your family), then you have no business overseeing the church. Does your family say, "Dad's always gone," or "My husband is always going and preaching somewhere," and do you respond, "What's wrong with you? You ought to give your life for the Lord. You ought to give up and realize that we've got to give our lives for God"? Well, giving your life is submitting to His lordship, and the Lord said to love your wife. The Lord said to teach your children. The Lord said to rule your home. That doesn't mean just to give commands and leave. If we rule our homes well, we're fit to oversee the house of God.

Chapter 24

The Servant's Heart

"But he that is greatest among you shall be your servant." (Matthew 23:11)

There's a spirit that's imbibed. I want to tell you something. My wife is the way she is because of her mother and her mother's mother, and it's gone to my daughter, and it will be found in her daughters. Can you thank God for the holy seed? Your children and your grandchildren are going to be what you are. They're going to be just as selfish as you are, just as manipulative as you are, and just as non-forgiving and compromising as you are, because you reap what you sow. What we're talking about here, beloved, is not just the immediate conflict that some of you find yourselves in, but what spirit you are bringing into the next generation. Are you showing them how to live?

Spiritual maturity is being able to serve. The greatest of all is the servant of all. Janet has been very ill these last eight or nine months, battling some stuff that is kind of new. For her to get up in the morning, just to get out of bed, is a chore. She doesn't just get out of bed in the morning. If the grandbabies are there, she gets out of bed and before she eats or does anything else, those babies are taken care of. They're fed and everybody else is taken care of.

We were at the races one day, a while back. It was kind of humorous. We were working on the cars when I looked down and saw Janet coming across the parking lot with boxes and bags, carrying everybody else's food. She brought food because she was concerned. Everybody had to get something to eat. I wasn't taken up with whether or not anybody ate, but there she was. She looked like a pack mule coming across the parking lot—the greatest among us.

"I'm so tired; I'm so weak. Would somebody run and get this for me, and would somebody do that for me? Please help me!" She has never acted like that, but models the fruit of the Spirit, the character of Christlikeness. She can't help herself; she has to serve other people. What's that all about? "Look not every man on his own thing, but every man also on the things of others."

During the years of our real popularity, we could have gone national or international with the ministry. At that particular time, you'd be surprised how many times Janet was asked to come speak at women's meetings. The perception at that time was that the preacher's wife should preach and teach and do all her stuff. Some were genuinely called, and for others it was a fad of team teaching, and there was no call on the lives of those individuals. They were just doing it because it was the fad. I've even had people ask me, "Well, why is it that your wife doesn't minister or doesn't want to minister?" I thought, "Dude, you don't have a clue what ministry is!" The fact that she doesn't get up here and parrot somebody else's teaching tape has nothing to do with ministry. Ministry is esteeming others better than yourself and looking to others, not vaunting yourself or wanting equal pulpit rights.

Chapter 25

Praying for Family Holiness

"Job...rose up early in the morning, and offered burnt offerings according to the number of them all: for Job said, It may be that my sons have sinned, and cursed God in their hearts. Thus did Job continually." (Job 1:5)

I pray a lot for my children, especially as they're older now, in these areas of coming to know why God has placed them as He has and who they are. God sovereignly put them into a family order. I pray that there would be the awareness and the fulfillment of whatever the call might be. I pray for their contentment in the areas of whatever their call and gifts are, that they would be at peace in who they are. My family situation is somewhat unique.

These are some of the practical things that I pray for the kids, to experience in their lives, and that it would work. Those are things that I try to pray about, but as a rule, I pray in great generality. I pray principles because I really believe that God has a better grasp than I do on what's going on and what they need. I pray a lot for them in the Spirit and with groanings that can't be uttered. If I can step back from my own prejudices and pray for them in the Spirit, it's going to benefit them more.

I thought it was humorous when Ronnie shared about one of the pastors in Africa really getting upset with him and Tera because Tera wouldn't come up and preach in the church. She said, "I don't want to," and Ron said, "She doesn't want to." They said, "She needs to come up and give us a word." He said, "No, she doesn't want to!" It's understanding, from the ministry aspect, how the wife fits. She isn't called; I'm called. She doesn't have to answer to the same things I'm answering to. My wife is not Mrs. Pastor. She's Mrs. Scott. She's my helpmeet, not yours. I pray that they would understand that role, because those are things they've had to go through over the years.

Chapter 26

Follow Me as I Follow Christ

"Be ye followers of me, even as I also am of Christ."
(1 Corinthians 11:1)

The more I obey, the more I want to obey. The clearer I can see, the freer I am from the appetite of sin in my members. We're purified by obeying the truth, the Word of God, through the Holy Spirit unto unfeigned love. I begin to live for others and serve others. I'm more concerned with others' edification than my own. I'm not preoccupied with self. I now realize that as a holy individual, a living stone, I've been placed here not for my worth, not for what I get out of it, but as a vessel so that I can contribute to others. I've become an instrument to edify others, to encourage others, to be an example of the believer.

There is a lot of talk in the world today about role models. People say, "I don't want to be a role model. I just want to be famous and have lots of money. I don't want to be responsible for my own actions." That's the exact opposite of what the church is. The apostle says, "Be followers of me. Follow me as I follow Christ." Be followers of those who through faith and patience are inheriting the promises of God.

It is our responsibility to set a course. Can I ask you a question? How many of you are confident enough to turn to people in your congregation, to your wife and children, and say, "If you follow me, you'll get to heaven. If you do what I do, you'll get to heaven. If you think what I think, if your heart is full of the same treasures as my heart, you're going to get to heaven"? That's what we need to do. Until we can say with confidence, "Follow me as I follow Christ," we are not properly representing our Head, Jesus. We need to examine our hearts and ask ourselves, "Am I really doing my job? Am I representing His lordship?"

Through the purifying of our souls, we begin to love one another and become role models who can say, "If you follow me, you're going to make it to heaven." What a responsibility. "I don't want that responsibility!" That's what God has called you to do, and then He gives you the grace and the strength to do it. Does that mean we're going to be perfect and never fail? Of course not, but we're able to do what? We're able to comfort with the same comfort wherewith we've been comforted. You say, "I know what you're going through, man! Yeah, I fight the same battles. I have the same problems with pride, jealously, selfishness, and slothfulness," or whatever it might be that you're battling in your life. We're all the same. Nobody here is free from the temptations and the "humanness" that we have from our father, Adam. Here we are, all battling in the same war, warring against all this ugliness in our flesh. We need each other. The Scripture says we are to lift up the hands that are hanging down, to comfort the feeble- minded."

Chapter 27

The True Man of God Is Blameless

"A bishop then must be blameless…" (1 Timothy 3:2)

In English, "blameless" means you've never done anything wrong. I'd have to leave right now, because I've made a bunch of mistakes. Even since becoming a Christian, I've made mistakes and have sinned. Even since becoming a pastor, I've made mistakes and sinned. We make mistakes; we're not blameless, but that's not what the Greek word means.

In the Greek, the word "blameless" is a very interesting word. It means "one that cannot be laid hold upon." What do you mean? What's that got to do with anything? There's another definition. It means "irreproachable." In other words, a reproach is not being brought on the ministry by our lives. The word "reproach" means "accusation." In other words, nobody can accuse you of doing wrong, of cheating others, of cheating on your wife. No one can accuse you of using worldly methods to bring the gospel. You're blameless. No one can lay hold on you.

Another meaning is that no one can censor you. Do you know what it means to "censor" somebody? It means to shut you up. In other words, nobody has anything against you that he can bring out to shut you up. There are no hidden things that, if anybody found out, could shut you up. If those hidden things are there, ultimately they're going to come out, and a reproach is going to be brought on the gospel. Then everybody's going to say, "I knew it! Those

Christians are no different than anybody else, especially those preachers. They're the biggest liars of all." That's what the world says about us. "Why would they say that? That's not nice." Probably because there's a lot of truth in it. I'm not talking about the true church. I'm talking about everybody that says he's a Christian and everybody that says he's a preacher, but brings a reproach. The true man of God is blameless.

Chapter 28

Holding to the Standard of Perfection

"And he gave some, apostles; and some, prophets; and some, evangelists; and some, pastors and teachers; For the perfecting of the saints..."
(Ephesians 4:11-12)

Pastors and teachers have some gifts in common. Evangelists and pastors have some gifts in common. Apostles and prophets have some gifts and responsibilities in common, but this is what all five have in common: these gifts were given by Jesus, number one, "for the perfecting of the saints." If your ministry has a standard lower than perfection, then God didn't send you. I'll say it again. If your ministry has a standard lower than perfection, then God did not send you; you're not His servant. If you have man's standards and not God's, Scripture makes it very clear what you're trusting in. The wisdom of man is foolishness with God.

Let me just share something with you about the wisdom of God. We all know that the wisdom of man is foolishness to God, but the wisdom of God is also foolishness to man. The Bible says that the carnal mind cannot receive the things of the Spirit of God, for they are foolishness to him. Carnal thinking is that which doesn't originate in the heart of God. I want you to hear something very clearly, because this will help you when I talk about "perfecting the saints." Just because something is good, doesn't mean it's God! We mistake morality and humanitarianism for Christianity, and they're not one and the same. They are two different kingdoms running parallel to each other.

We know that the fear of the Lord is the beginning of wisdom. We also understand that there's a wisdom that came from the fruit in the midst of the Garden, which was knowledge of good and evil. What was it that caused Adam and Eve to partake of that fruit? Listen to what was said: "Eat that fruit. In the day ye eat thereof, then your eyes shall be opened, and ye shall be as gods, knowing good and evil. You'll have the ability to know good from evil." The warfare being dealt with in the Garden was between absolute dependence on God and independence (what we know, how we can apply truth and laws, etc.). I used the words "independence" and "dependence." This is what we're trying to do in perfecting our people: to make them totally dependent upon God. This is important because this is the original sin. Do you want to know what the definition of true humility is? True humility is absolute dependence upon God.

What was it that the Lord was trying to speak to His people and prepare us for in this hour? There is a remnant throughout the world of the true church of Jesus Christ. This highway of holiness that we're walking on is a straight gate and a narrow way. There are a lot of professed "preachers," but very few holy men that are called of God. When we talk about holy, it's those that are set apart for God. I don't just mean that you're working for God; I mean that God is your only source. The deception in the minds of so many people is that America is the answer. America is not the answer; God is the answer. Amen? If you're going to be the shepherds after God's own heart, the lordship of Jesus Christ is what you're going to have to infuse into the hearts of the people in your congregations. They're going to have to see that they're not an inferior people. They are a holy people, a peculiar people, that are set apart to bring praise to God through lives that are holy.

Chapter 29

Nothing More Frightening Than Perfection

"But the Lord said unto me, Say not, I am a child: for thou shalt go to all that I shall send thee, and whatsoever I command thee thou shalt speak. Be not afraid of their faces: for I am with thee to deliver thee, saith the Lord." (Jeremiah 1:7-8)

I read in Jeremiah that if I fear men's faces, I will be confounded before them. Do you know what Jeremiah, Chapter one, says? When God sent him forth to preach, he said, "I can't go out there. I'm a child; I can't speak." God said, "I have sent you," then He put the coal on Jeremiah's lips to sanctify them and sent him forth. Then he preached the Word as a hammer that broke the rock in pieces—fearful in the beginning, invincible in the end.

There's nothing more frightening than talking to your church about being perfect. Do you know why? A lot of them may not like that standard. They'll go down the street to the other church where the standards aren't so high—which means your offerings have gone down, so now you have to eat fewer beans. Now the perception of your worth has gone down in the community. You used to have a big church of one hundred, and now you've got twenty-five. "You know what? There must be sin in that church!" becomes the gossip of the neighborhood. "That's why they're not growing. If they were a biblical church, God would be blessing them." "I've got to keep these people here. I've got to keep them happy. I know what the

Bible says about that area, but I'm just going to have to tone it down a little bit."

As we make a stand—not on our emotions, but on the declared will of God—we can speak, and it doesn't matter what anybody has to say. What I could not do with thirty thousand people I can now do with three hundred. Is that the message of Gideon? Then let's raise the standard in our churches to perfection. Let's start looking for the people. I'm looking for three hundred warriors. I'm looking for three hundred people who aren't afraid of what men can do to them, three hundred young Davids who'll take a stone and go forth, not in the world's methods of Saul with his armor.

Chapter 30

Laying Your Life down for the Sheep

"I am the good shepherd: the good shepherd giveth his life for the sheep." (John 10:11)

We're talking about shepherding God's flock and what our job is, your responsibility and mine. The Scripture says that the Good Shepherd does something. What is it? What is one of the first things we have to do? Lay down our lives for the sheep. Does that mean we're supposed to do everything for the people? That is not what that means. Laying down your life for the sheep means that you do what is not natural: you're willing to die to yourself. You're willing to have people get upset. You're willing to have people misunderstand. You're willing to have the sheep maybe even say among themselves periodically, "I don't know if he has us on a good path today or not. What do you think?" Can you see some sheep walking along and saying, "I don't know…I don't see anything to eat. Do you?" "Well, I don't know." "Does anybody see any water?"

The shepherd knows where he is going. He knows where the still waters are. He knows where the green pastures are. Once you begin to show your people that you know where God is and you know how to access the presence and the power of God, they'll follow you. Do you want to know what it means to lay your life down for the sheep? It means that you need to start dying to yourself and stop making life easy on yourself. Your prayer, your study, and your application of the Word of God begin to build confidence in the peoples' hearts.

When you read these Scriptures, you begin to see what your responsibility is in putting the house of God in order. I may have gotten some of you in trouble. You're going to go back and say, "Praise God, I've studied and that's the Word," and your people are going to put a knot on your head, but don't faint! Don't fear their faces. Love them better than you love yourself. Be a good shepherd; die to self for the flock, and God will honor you.

Chapter 31

Lead Your People to Holiness

"For the perfecting of the saints, for the work of
the ministry, for the edifying of the body of Christ."
(Ephesians 4:12)

Your responsibility is to perfect the saints. That word "perfect"
means "to be brought to completion or maturity." It's not the
false doctrine of sinless perfection. Some of you may have heard
that. Over the years there have been groups that have taught the
doctrine of sinless perfection. They teach that there is a second
work of grace, and that, from that moment of "sanctification," they
never sin again. "I am sanctified and from that moment on, I never
will sin again." Well, you just sinned by saying that because now
you're lying! I could follow you for fifteen minutes and catch you
sinning. This doctrine of sinless perfection was created because of
a misunderstanding of biblical sanctification. Sanctification is a
process. They wanted to be sanctified. Their motives were right. They
wanted to be holy before God, but their methods were wrong. They
didn't understand sanctification. Sanctification is not an instantaneous
work; it's a process. We're being sanctified and will be sanctified until
we're glorified. At that moment—then and only then—sin is no longer
a power or force in our members that we have to contend with.

When I say "perfection," don't think that I'm saying the people in
our churches have to be perfect in a sinless manner. They have to
be perfect in their pursuits. A "perfect" man is one who is perfectly
pursuing God. It doesn't matter where he is on the scale of our

perceived holiness—and we all have those scales. What you think is holy might be different from what I think is holy. We call that "conscience." You need to realize that conscience is a whole different subject than holiness. We have liberty in our consciences. We can all be led into different areas of conscience, but we're all static, or the same, in our perception of holiness. It's the same standard for everybody.

Let me define holiness for you. "Holiness" is a term that you're very familiar with, and it has to do with all of the Old Testament types of consecration: the utensils of worship that were consecrated, the table of shewbread, the laver that they washed their hands in, and the altar of incense. These things were "consecrated," or "holy." The word means "set apart for God only." In other words, the spoon that you dipped in the incense at the temple can't be taken home to eat with; it's only for God.

God has called you to lead your people to holiness. Our job is to get them to see that they are only for God, not for the world, not to make a better living, not to provide for their children to go to college, but to make sure that their household is only for God. For us as pastors, this is not an easy job. Even though people may be regenerated, new creatures, there's still that gravitation toward the world because of the sin that's in our members. Every one of us is drawn into the world. Every one of us wants life easier on our flesh. Every one of us has physical appetites that we want to pursue. "Lust" means "the inability to control," and "an uncontrollable appetite." All that's in the world is the lust of the flesh, the lust of the eyes, and the pride of life. That's what we're warring in our churches. Every time you stand up to preach the gospel, you're warring against those three things that are in the church: the lust of the flesh, the lust of the eyes, and the pride of life.

Chapter 32

Requiring a Holy Life

"…Unto a perfect man, unto the measure of the stature of the fulness of Christ: That we henceforth be no more children, tossed to and fro, and carried about with every wind of doctrine…" (Ephesians 4:13-14)

We have a few people telling everybody, "You need to grow up!" It isn't done in a harsh way, but in the biblical demand that says, "Look, God has called us to perfection." Many of these things that you keep bothering people with, you need to be praying about. You need to be studying for yourself, to show yourself a workman that needeth not be ashamed. It's not written just to Timothy.

He says we're to minister in this way: "Till we all come in the unity of the faith, and of the knowledge of the Son of God, unto a perfect man, unto the measure of the stature of the fulness of Christ: That we henceforth [this is very important] be no more children, tossed to and fro, and carried about with every wind of doctrine, by the sleight of men, and cunning craftiness, whereby they lie in wait to deceive: But speaking the truth in love, may grow up into him in all things, which is the head, even Christ" (verses 13-15). Beloved, this is the requirement, so when a visiting pastor comes to town and starts pushing people down, mimicking the work of the Holy Spirit, your congregation doesn't think that's what you're supposed to do. When an evangelist comes to town and tells your people that everybody in the church is supposed to be rich, you've established enough of a doctrine that they're not tossed to and fro, and they understand the Scriptures because you're requiring of them a holy life. It's very important that we understand these things. If we don't—Listen! I'm talking to you as pastors—the blood is going to be on your hands. We are the watchmen who stand and declare the sword of the Lord, or the judgment, that is at hand! If we don't declare what false doctrine can do in the lives of the congregation and in the lives of brothers and sisters in the ministry, then the blood is going to be on our hands.

If we're going to protect people from false doctrine, then we need to have sound doctrine, don't we? Do you know what I'd like to encourage some of you to do? You'll think this is strange. One of your jobs is to make your church as small as you can get it. It's a straight path, and few there be that find it. It's very unusual to have large—and "large" is relative—organizations without mingled seed. It's very difficult.

The thing that will protect you as an overseer, as your ministry grows and gets larger, is the standard that you keep. I would much rather have a large church of perfect people than a small church of perfect people; but I'd also rather have a small church of perfect people than a large church of carnal people. You can get more done with Gideon's three hundred. Send the fearful ones home, and let's go to battle! If God is for us, who can be against us? I shared with you, practically, one of the things we experienced at home. We lost a thousand people in a very short period of time, and our income went up—and we doubled our missions giving! That tells me that all of those people were parasites. Study the Scriptures and see if God doesn't refine and try to reduce to the lowest common denominator of righteousness. Let's stop being seduced by the world's standard of success into thinking that "more" or "big" is better. Holy is better. Mighty is better.

Chapter 33

Sheep on Steroids

"That there should be no schism in the body; but that the members should have the same care one for another." (1 Corinthians 12:25)

Corinthians says the church is to have the same care one for another. The church is to be interwoven to where they are supporting and lifting up the hands that hang down and encouraging one another. It's your job to train them and feed them so they are not fearful and they are not dismayed and they are not lacking. How healthy is your flock?

Do any of you know what steroids are? A steroid is a substance that athletes and body builders use to make their muscles grow much faster than normal. Our congregation is sheep on steroids. If a wolf comes into our flock, our sheep can kill it, because they are stronger than wolves. Those are the kind of sheep we need to start raising. If a wolf comes into our flock, it's dangerous. Do you know that every time there are visitors, they cannot leave without people coming around and saying, "Hey, how are you doing?" and trying to minister to them? They will bring them sound doctrine. If they see someone out of order, they will reprove him, rebuke him, and instruct him in righteousness. You don't even want to step out of line in our church. Those folks will jump you, jealous for the gospel and for the holiness of God. I love it; I love our people. It is a great place to be. They love God, and they love the Word of God. If you're a preacher, they'll wear you out. They will sit and listen and take notes until you collapse.

Chapter 34

Find Your Young Timothys

"And the things that thou hast heard of me among many witnesses, the same commit thou to faithful men, who shall be able to teach others also." (2 Timothy 2:2)

That's what we're really supposed to be doing in each one of our ministries: finding faithful men that we can pour our lives into. Isn't that what Jesus did? He found twelve and emptied Himself into them. He did minister to the masses periodically, but His life was given to twelve men who turned the world upside down. That's the principle that God has called us to walk in. You see it when Jethro, Moses' father-in-law, came to him and said, "You're wearing out yourself and the people." How many of you remember that? Moses was doing everything. He was hearing all the problems in the church, and he was giving the counsel. The Scripture says that from morning until evening, he sat and heard all of these different problems. Jethro said, "This isn't wise." What did they do? They chose out an eldership, men who were full of the Holy Ghost who could begin to oversee this. Then Moses said, "Bring the difficult matters to me." This is the wisdom of God.

We see it flowing into the New Testament, don't we? When the church began to grow beyond the apostolic oversight, the individual oversight, what happened? They began to choose out men full of the Holy Ghost whom they ordained as deacons. We want to talk a little bit about our role in building the church. What is your responsibility as the gift of God—called of God and placed, as the Scripture says, as it pleased Him? The first responsibility you have is to find people among you that are faithful, that you can begin to commit to, and who are able to teach others also. You need to find your young Timothys, your sons in the faith. You need to find the aged men that are wise, that you can count on. Your ministry will never grow beyond the foundation that you build in finding faithful men, in pouring your life into them to assume the ministry. The reason most of us don't do that is because we're so afraid and insecure that they might become better than we are. I have people on my staff that are better than I am in all kinds of areas. If they weren't, they wouldn't be on my staff. I wouldn't need them if I could do it myself. What is our standard, the standard for all of us? The perfecting of the saints. The standard for your church is perfection—nothing else can be tolerated—perfect in pursuit, hearts that are perfect in panting after God.

Chapter 35

Perfecting Your Men in the Mundane

"Then the twelve called the multitude of the disciples unto them, and said, It is not reason that we should leave the word of God, and serve tables." (Acts 6:2)

Don't let your deacons be limited to mundane tasks. Bring them to the place where they can begin to counsel with the Word of God. Bring them to the place where they can begin to speak wisdom into hearts, just as Moses was able to use those elders so that he didn't have to deal with every issue. We've trained our deacons at home to the point where every one of our deacons could pastor a church with no problem; but they're not called to that. You don't graduate from deacon to elder. It's not a promotion. There's nothing inferior about the office of deacon if that is where God has placed you. We see one evolution of it, don't we? Who was a deacon that became a five-fold ministry gift? Philip, the evangelist. We realize that God can reach in and touch one of these hearts and move them into a five-fold ministry position. Primarily, though, they're serving the local church, waiting on the tables.

Somebody in the church is in need of prayer; they're physically sick, and they're in need of prayer. Do you call the pastor? You have a need. The Scripture says if you're sick to call on the elders of the church, right? They can anoint you with oil. You can call, because this is a true ministry of eldership.

What if I have need of food? "We don't have any food." Do I call the pastor? Whom do I call? I call a deacon, and I say, "We're in a situation here. We don't have food; we don't have provision." This man then prayerfully represents this need to the overseers—the mundane things. What about counseling? What about marital problems? What about all of the other things that are involved in ministry? The ministry belongs to the church.

Listen. If you don't hear anything else, understand this: God is calling you to perfect men so you don't have to do many of those things that you're spending your time doing now. This is so that you can pray and study to bring a more in-depth word to your people, to stand before them, and to expect of them a greater degree of holiness.

Chapter 36

Will Your Ministry Die with You?

> "And Joshua the son of Nun was full of the spirit of wisdom; for Moses had laid his hands upon him: and the children of Israel hearkened unto him, and did as the Lord commanded Moses." (Deuteronomy 34:9)

As the man of God looking for these Timothys, look for faithful men, not talented men. The requirement of a steward, the Scripture says, is that he be found what? Faithful. That is the greatest quality in serving. The man of God is looking across the congregations and in his travels for men that are faithful. Faithful to what? Well, Elisha wasn't looking for a position. He was just pouring water over the hands of the prophet, and yet the mantle fell on him. You never know whom the mantle will fall on. You don't just pour water to get the mantle. You pour water because you're a servant. Then God chooses whom He's going to ordain and raise to another capacity, but every one of us needs to have a servant's heart.

The necessity of choosing a Timothy is seen in the lives of Moses and Joshua. Somebody had to carry on the vision and get the people to the Promised Land. If you have a heart as a man of God for your flock, it's not enough for you just to teach them, instruct them, provide for them, and then die, leaving the church without any oversight. Paul said, "I have no one else that I can commend to you that has the same faith and the same heart as my son, Timothy."

That's what it's all about, being able to commend to another generation and say, "Even when I'm gone, this is the gift of God still working in your lives." It was taken from Moses and conferred upon Joshua. Hands were laid upon Timothy by the presbytery; gifts were given to him by prophecy of the apostle, and it carried on. Is your ministry going to die with you, or do you have someone that's being raised up to lead that next generation into the Promised Land?